FRUIT OF THE SPIRIT

FOR YOUNG DISCIPLES

By Karajah Yashar

Orlando, FL 2024

www.BSPBooks.com

ISBN: 978-1-962691-41-3

First Edition: August 2024

Table of Contents

The Fruit of Love......................3

The Fruit of Joy......................5

The Fruit of Peace......................7

The Fruit of Patience...................9

The Fruit of Kindness...............11

The Fruit of Goodness.............13

The Fruit of Faithfulness...........15

The Fruit of Gentleness............17

The Fruit of Self Control..........19

THE FRUIT OF LOVE

Love, one of the fruits of the Spirit, means caring for others in a way that is kind and selfless. Imagine how you feel when someone shares their toys with you or helps you when you're upset. That's the kind of love God wants us to show. It's not just about saying "I love you," but about doing things that make others feel special and valued, just like how Jesus loved our people and showed kindness and care to people around Him.

When we show love, we help others feel happy and important. It's like being a good friend who always listens and helps when needed. Love means putting others first and being patient, even when it's hard. Just as Jesus loved us so much that He did wonderful things and even made sacrifices, we can try to show that same kind of love in our own lives by being kind, helpful, and understanding to everyone around us.

THE FRUIT OF JOY

Joy, one of the fruits of the Spirit, is about feeling really happy and excited inside, even when things aren't perfect. It's like when you're having fun playing with friends or celebrating a special occasion. But joy is more than just having fun; it's a deep and lasting happiness that comes from knowing that God loves us and is always with us. Even on tough days, joy helps us stay positive and appreciate the good things in life.

When we have joy, we share that happiness with others. It's like spreading sunshine wherever we go, making people smile and feel good. Joy helps us stay thankful and find something to be happy about, even when things aren't going our way. By being joyful, we show that we trust God and believe that He has good plans for us, helping us shine brightly and make the world a happier place.

THE FRUIT OF PEACE

Peace is a special feeling of calm and quiet inside, even when things around us might be noisy or confusing. It's like having a cozy spot in your heart where you feel safe and relaxed. When you have peace, you're not worried or upset, and you know that everything will be okay because God is looking after you. It's the calm you feel when you take a deep breath and remember that God is with you, even if things don't go as planned.

Sharing peace with others means helping everyone feel calm and happy too. It's like when you help your friends solve a problem or when you're kind to someone who's feeling sad. Peace helps us get along with others and make sure everyone feels good. When we have peace, we can be a calming and comforting presence for our friends and family, showing them that God's love helps us stay calm and happy no matter what's happening around us.

THE FRUIT OF PATIENCE

Patience is about waiting without getting upset or angry. Imagine you're really excited to go to a friend's party, but you have to wait until the weekend. Patience helps you wait with a happy heart instead of feeling frustrated. It's like when you plant a seed in the ground—it takes time to grow into a beautiful flower, and you can't rush it. Being patient means you trust that good things are coming, even if they take a little while.

God gives us patience so we can handle situations where we need to wait or when things don't happen right away. Just like when you wait your turn in a game or when you're waiting for your favorite dessert to be ready, patience helps you stay calm and happy. It's a special way to show love to others and to trust that everything will work out in the right time.

THE FRUIT OF KINDNESS

Kindness is all about being nice and caring to the people around you. Imagine you see someone who dropped their books—kindness is when you go over to help them pick everything up with a smile. It's like sharing your toys with a friend or giving a compliment to make someone feel good. God wants us to show kindness because it makes the world a happier place for everyone.

When you're kind, you make others feel loved and special. Even small acts, like saying "thank you" or helping your parents set the table, are ways to show kindness. It's like being a light that brightens someone's day. Kindness is one of the ways we can show that we care about others, just like God cares about us.

11

FRUIT OF GOODNESS

Goodness is about doing the right thing, even when it's not easy. Imagine your friend's bike is broken, and they don't know how to fix it. Showing goodness means offering to help them, even if it takes time and effort. When you choose to do good, like helping a friend fix their bike, you're not just making their day better—you're doing what makes God happy, too.

Being good also means thinking about how your actions affect others. If you see someone struggling, like your friend with the broken bike, showing goodness means stepping in to help, even if you have other things to do. Goodness is like planting seeds of kindness that grow into big, beautiful trees of happiness, making the world a better place for everyone around you.

THE FRUIT OF FAITHFULNESS

Faithfulness is about being someone people can trust. Imagine you promised your friend you'd help them study for a big test. Even if you feel like playing video games instead, being faithful means keeping your promise and helping them out. When you're faithful, you show others that they can count on you, just like we can always count on God to keep His promises.

Being faithful also means sticking by your friends and family, even when things get tough. If your friend is going through a hard time, faithfulness means staying by their side and supporting them. It's about being loyal, just like how God is always with us no matter what. When you practice faithfulness, you build strong relationships and show that you're a dependable and loving person.

15

FRUIT OF GENTLENESS

Gentleness is about being kind, soft, and careful with your words and actions. Imagine you're holding a tiny baby kitten—you wouldn't squeeze it or be rough with it because you know it's delicate and needs to be handled with care. That's what gentleness is like with people too. When you speak gently, you choose kind words that don't hurt others' feelings. You listen patiently and treat others with care, showing them that they're important to you.

Being gentle also means helping others in a way that makes them feel safe and loved. For example, if a friend is feeling sad, you might gently put your arm around them and offer comforting words. Gentleness isn't about being weak; it's about using your strength to help and protect others in a loving way. When you practice gentleness, you make the world a softer, kinder place for everyone around you.

THE FRUIT OF SELF CONTROL

Self-control is like having a superpower that helps you make good choices, even when it's hard. Imagine you're at a party, and there's a big table full of cookies and candy. It's easy to want to eat everything, but self-control helps you decide to eat just one or two treats instead of overloading on sweets. Self-control also means waiting patiently, like standing in line for your turn at a game or to be called to go play outside. It helps you stay calm and not rush ahead, even if you're excited.

Self-control also means staying calm when you feel upset or angry. Let's say your little brother or sister takes your favorite toy without asking. Instead of shouting or grabbing it back, self-control helps you take a deep breath, stay calm, and talk about it kindly. By practicing self-control, you learn to handle your feelings and actions in a way that keeps you out of trouble and helps you get along better with others. It's an important part of growing up and making smart choices every day.

19

www.ingramcontent.com/pod-product-compliance
Lightning Source LLC
Chambersburg PA
CBHW081016120626
46546CB00010B/3174